GRACE FILLED PLATES:

A 30-DAY DEVOTIONAL

BRANDICE LARDNER

CONTENTS

Free Prayer Printable

Wanna add some prayer power to your devotional time?

Download your free companion prayer printable at:

www.GraceFilledPlate.com/GFP-Prayers

INTRODUCTION

HEEEEEYYYY! You're here and I'm so excited to meet you!

Although we just met, I know that we're going to become fast friends. That's what happens when two people have so much in common.

Because, if you picked up this book, you get it. You get what it's like to try to "fix" your life by trying to lose weight. You know what it's like to think that the solution to your problems is yet another diet, only to see that it, too, leaves you feeling worse than the last.

I get it. I was there too.

And, I'm here to share with great joy that *ditching all that diet baggage is possible*!

What follows in these pages is a discovery of how **God's grace can transform your relationship with food.** As you read and absorb (and do your Grace in Action steps), you'll begin to feel the food guilt lift. Ahhh…

And, I bet you'll be pleasantly surprised how this change of focus can actually fuel the healthy habits you've been longing to make.

Are you ready?

Awesome! Then, it's time to dive into Day 1.

Oh, *before you start*, let's remember that this journey is All. About. Grace. So, keep an eye out for the knee-jerk reaction of turning this into just another "diet." There's no "good" or "bad," "off" or "on." There's only today and what we decide to do with it.

Take the 30 days at your own pace. Some of the devos have deep questions and thoughtful action points, so don't rush.

If you miss a week, come back when you can. In doing so, you'll be ditching the all-or-nothing thinking and proving that you're doing this because it matters to you (and God!).

Ok, friend, I think we're ready now!

DAY 1: THE SINKING SHIP

VERSE: *For I do not understand my own actions. For I do not do what I want, but I do the very thing I hate.* Romans 7:15 ESV

READ: Romans 7:15-25

"I HATE THIS! Why can't I stop?" I exclaimed in my mind as I helplessly ate the last corner of the 3rd cookie I was sneaking (after I'd planned on not having any).

There was a war waging within my soul and I felt torn by my choices like Dr. Jekyll and Mr. Hyde. "What's wrong with me?! I know this will make me miserable, and yet, I still do it..." I contemplated eating more since I already blew it today, all while vowing to do better (no, perfect) tomorrow.

My ship was sinking. Fast.

Have you ever noticed that even a deep desire to do better has little to no impact on certain sticky behaviors that we cling to? For some, it may be shopping or having a glass of wine (or 3) after dinner. For you and me, it may be food.

Whatever our struggle, we hold on to it like a lifesaver — all the while that "red and white circle" is actually made of cement.

While I'm not one for making excuses, I think we'd all benefit from looking at our reasons: Why do you turn to excess food when it's causing you so much pain? What are you trying to escape that's making food look like a necessary evil?

Try to dig beneath the surface and see what propels you. Then, take that desire, hurt, or pain to the Lord in prayer. And if you're lost for insight, don't sweat it. Even Paul was unable to comprehend why he'd stray from the Lord.

GRACE IN ACTION:

Today, before you take that unnecessary bite, pause and ask the Holy Spirit to reveal what's driving you to the food. Then, say a short prayer asking God to take you one step closer to a better solution.

DAY 2: PRAY FOR DIRECTION

VERSE: *And your ears shall hear a word behind you, saying, "This is the way, walk in it," when you turn to the right or when you turn to the left.* Isaiah 30:21 ESV

READ: Isaiah 30:18-22

"LORD, SHOULD I MARRY HIM?" "Should I take the job?" "Should we buy the house?"

Big decisions and uncertain situations. When our direction is unclear, our first line of defense is often to seek the Lord. While His voice isn't audible, the Holy Spirit stamps His welcome direction in our hearts.

Some call it "gut instinct," but we know it's more than last night's chili. God cares about where we go and promises to lead us along the way.

But, what about the little, seemingly insignificant things. You know, simple things like whether you should: go see a movie or stay in; visit your neighbor or call a friend; eat or not eat that last cookie lingering on the kitchen counter.

Can you really expect Holy Navigation in these forgettable choices?

Yes, you can!

How many times will you choose a spouse, take a new job, or buy a new home? And, how many times will you decide whether or not to eat or drink to the glory of God (1 Corinthians 10:31)?

We're talking a dozen decisions compared to a quarter of a million+. Not only is our God relational and wanting to be involved in your daily life, He also cares about the state of your heart and body. How you eat can be an excellent indicator of both.

So, yes. You can **ask** *and* **expect** to hear Him saying, "This is the way [eat or don't eat it]."

The problem is that we often plow ahead without thinking, either unaware or unwilling to hear a possible "stop" signal. That's the product of a dieting past. A book dictating what you eat-- and an internal defense protecting what feels taken away.

> **But God's ways are higher. Don't put Him in a diet box.**

He doesn't want to deprive you or leave you helpless in a stew of negative emotions. Even Jesus was considered a glutton by onlookers because of His enjoyment of food.

4

You can trust God with how you eat. Are you willing to ask and listen?

GRACE IN ACTION:

At least once before or while you're eating today, pause and ask the Lord to show you what **He** would have. Then, put your faith into your food choice and obey His voice, sowing a seed of self-control.

DAY 3: SOWING SEEDS

VERSE: *Do not be deceived: God is not mocked, for whatever one sows, that will he also reap.* Galatians 6:7 ESV

READ: Galatians 6:7-10

MY HUSBAND IS A FAR BETTER gardener than I, but even "green thumbs" make mistakes. We stood admiring a bountiful batch of tomato seedlings he'd grown. So small and delicate, it was hard to imagine these little "trees" ever bearing great fruit.

He decided to share the harvest and potted up one of the larger babies to take to his mom. She was thrilled, and she carefully transferred and cared for her new plant.

A few weeks went by and we discovered something unexpected...the harvest would never come as she'd been nurturing a weed. Oops! We don't always think about the kinds of seeds we're planting, but the Bible tells us that our actions are sowing the potential for future growth, positive or otherwise.

Have you ever planted seeds that turned out to be weeds or something even worse? Maybe you knew what was happening or maybe you could plead innocence.

Either way, the spiritual law of sowing and reaping still stands like gravity. Cause and effect.

Praise God He doesn't require us to come with anything more than a seed.

What are you lacking in your walk with food? Do you long for more self-control, or do you know that everything would change if you could only be more consistent?

Then, it's time to sow a seed!

What is your mustard seed of faith(Matthew 13:31-32)? You can self-control by saying "no" to that extra bite and then watering it by praying for it to grow. Nurture seeds of consistency by committing to one small change today and tomorrow. And keep recommitting to bear fruit.

I believe that one of our biggest barriers to change is our ability to overcomplicate things and to push for perfectionism. Rather than getting caught up in the "shoulds," think about the "do's." What CAN you do TODAY?

GRACE IN ACTION:

Make a healthy choice today... but not because it will lead to weight loss. Rather, choose to sow a seed to reap a harvest of the fruit of the Spirit.

DAY 4: FEELING LIKE A FAILURE?

VERSE: *But he said to me, "My grace is sufficient for you, for my power is made perfect in weakness." Therefore I will boast all the more gladly of my weaknesses, so that the power of Christ may rest upon me.* 2 Corinthians 12:9 ESV

READ: 2 Corinthians 12:8-10

EVERYWHERE I LOOKED, I saw my failures. Dinner was burnt. I missed an important appointment. And I'd left the clothes in the washer and now they smelled like the ocean floor.

My eyes were keen for my shortcomings. Wherever I went, there they were.

I'd pretty much resigned to being a failure when it came to how I ate. I'd set the bar high, hoping that by shooting for the moon,

I'd land among the stars. And yet-- each day ended with regret as I laid my head on my pillow recounting all my food failures.

How am I to boast in the very weaknesses that seem to devalue my worth? The weaknesses that make me want to hide in shame?

When we attach our value to our behavior, we're headed for a rocky ride. Just as our early marriage will be tumultuous if we're only happy when our husbands meet our perfectionistic standards, so will our relationship with ourselves.

Accepting our faults is not meant to be a license-- but an invitation. When we can recognize our inability to meet our calling to holiness, we see the cavern between us and God that only He can fill.

Your struggles with food do not define you, but your reliance on God to overcome them will transform you.

How many times a day do you think about what to eat, what diet you should do, or how you wish your body looked? These are each an opportunity to fellowship with the Creator of the Universe. And, within that fellowship lives your freedom.

We boast in our weakness with double-chocolate brownies because it moves us to prayer and praise, two things that will make over any woman who is willing to do them!

GRACE IN ACTION:

Today, when you notice a weak point, stop any self-condemning thoughts and take them to God in prayer. Then praise Him for the power of Christ that will rest upon you!

DAY 5: WHY DIETS DON'T WORK

VERSE: *"Do not handle, Do not taste, Do not touch." These have indeed an appearance of wisdom... but they are of no value in stopping the indulgence of the flesh.* Colossians 2:21, 23 ESV

READ: Colossians 2:21-23

"I CAN'T EAT THAT," you said as you pushed the plate of cookies back across the table, so that the sight and chocolate aroma were blocked by your steaming cup of black coffee.

But, you wanted that cookie. Really wanted it. In fact, you were even a little distracted as the conversation progressed. Your best friend's son got a bad grade in English. Or was that math?

You skipped the cookie. And that was supposed to make you feel good about yourself, but then you couldn't let the thought go. Your sweet tooth was parched and   seeing a "sugary mirage" as you sat at the stop light directly across from Dunkin' Donuts.

You arrived home and the cookie monster was let loose. But, with no cookies to eat, cereal and crackers would have to do. You're not sure how many you ate, but looking back, you know it far exceeded that of one solitary, gooey cookie.

When we tap into worldly wisdom and say "no" to our cravings simply because we think we should, or because we want to shed some unwanted pounds, we're not actually solving our problems.

Our flesh is still panting for what it wants.

Diets don't work because they attempt to put a band-aid on why we're eating in the first place. Our desires and wants still exist, but they've been "prettied up" by our outward behavior.

But, like trying to keep a beach ball underwater, those cravings POP! back up.

The way to truly "fix" the problem of overindulgence is not a diet. The solution is found in meeting those true needs with true solutions. God's solutions.

- Stress eating is solved by God's peace.
- Comfort eating requires The Comforter.
- Boredom eating is alleviated by living His great purpose.
- Our Heavenly Father offers the medicine we need to soothe our food wounds.

GRACE IN ACTION:

Today, when you feel the desire to eat outside of hunger, pause and see what you really need. Ask yourself, "What is this food promising me?" Or fill in the blanks of "I'm afraid that if I don't eat, ____ will happen."

DAY 6: GOD'S GRACE MEANS YOU'RE GOOD ENOUGH

VERSE: *Therefore, if anyone is in Christ, he is a new creation. The old has passed away; behold, the new has come.* 2 Corinthians 5:17 ESV

READ: 2 Corinthians 5:14-17

YOU'RE WAITING ON SOMETHING. The door is open, but you hesitate to walk through because you're waiting for that something to be "just right."

Maybe you don't know it, or maybe you've intentionally put parts of your life on hold.

"If I can just lose this weight, *then* I'll be happy."

"Once I get my eating on track, *then* I'll feel good about myself."

"If only my kids would behave perfectly, *then* I'd love them."

Wait, what?

While we may long for a white picket fence in our dreams, we know that real life is peppered with struggles. People are people, and kids spill their milk on our freshly mopped floors. The thought of our love being shaken by their imperfect behavior is unthinkable.

Life's ups and downs may steal your joy some days, but they don't rock what you know matters most....your faith, your family, and your values. Those stick like super glue.

So, why is it that you hold peace and joy with food and your body at arm's length?

Why is it that you can't get past your imperfections and mop up that spilled milk?

B.C. (before Christ), you were held to a standard of holiness that you could never fulfill. But, after you accepted His grace and made Him Lord of your life, you (by His blood) filled every single standard God has set for your life.

You are, as they say-- "good to go."

But you and I, we still hang on to that worldly measuring stick where how we eat and whether or not we're bathing suit ready defines our worthiness.

It's as if Christ's sacrifice means nothing at all.

Ouch! Am I the only one on the verge of losing her lunch reading that?

Putting our lives on hold, waiting until we're "just right," is like walking around with a pocketful of

money, afraid to spend it because we don't believe it's real.

It is.

This message isn't meant to condemn you, but to inspire you to live like you were bought with a price. Today, you can start walking the walk of a new creation and, if I were a betting woman, I'd say you'd start feeling like one.

GRACE IN ACTION:

What is holding you back from walking in the fullness of Christ? Today, when you feel yourself shrinking back because of your shortcomings, put your foot down on that negative thought and stand on the blood of Christ!

DAY 7: COZY IN HIS LAP

VERSE: *Not that I have already obtained this or am already perfect, but I press on to make it my own, because Christ Jesus has made me his own.* Philippians 3:12 ESV

READ: Philippians 3:12-16

MY COLLECTION of diet books had exceeded capacity. There wasn't room for one more "solution." I dusted them off as I loaded them into a box to donate. Each one bringing memories of a hope and failure all their own.

I'm grateful to be past the point of looking for a solution to all of my life's problems in a diet book. Those bygone attempts were only sandpaper to my already wounded soul, as I felt as if I'd let God down each binge-y bite.

Sigh.

But underneath all those pages of failure lived something I neglected to recognize. A quality I'd neglected to celebrate. I think you do too.

You and I, we're resilient. Yes, we've fallen more times than we can count, but each and every time we get back up.

Don't count how many days you've spent with your face in the mud. God doesn't.

Rather, think of how God must be glad that you're willing to keep fighting to please Him. Just as it touches your heart when even a disobedient child finds comfort sitting on your lap, so God longs to comfort us. But He can only do so when we let Him.

Not a single one of us will do this thing called "life" perfectly. But, we CAN keep bringing our gaze back to The One who gave up everything for our sake.

GRACE IN ACTION:

Imagine a recent episode where you started down a slippery food slope. Picture the scene.

Now, how could you rewrite that story so that you ended up in the comfort of God's "lap"?

Create a plan of action for the next time you're face-first in a food temptation.

DAY 8: THE ALLURE OF WEIGHT LOSS

VERSE: *So, whether you eat or drink, or whatever you do, do all to the glory of God.* 1 Corinthians 10:31 ESV

READ: 1 Corinthians 10:24-31

AM I the only one who's drawn to before and after weight-loss pictures like a moth to the light? Something about them is like a Pixy Stixs for my flesh. The subject, standing proudly (at just the right angle, of course) boasting of her great accomplishment.

"How did she do it?" I used to wonder, scouring her story for information I'd hoped I could reproduce. I'm not sure what was more alluring to me-- the weight loss itself or the queried attention it created.

Either way, my focus was laser and it was on ME.

Why do you want to lose weight? What about a shrinking size leaves you starstruck?

God does great things in us and for us because of His kingdom purpose. He has a grand plan in mind that is far greater than a jeans size. Even the most daily tasks have the capacity to glorify God. Why would weight loss be any different?

> *If you're wondering why your weight-loss efforts have stalled, stop and consider if God can bless your "why."*

What does true health and wellness mean to you and your circle of influence? How do they fit into your calling?

I'm not suggesting that you alter your goals so that they "qualify" for God's blessing, but that you pause to examine what you really value in life. What characteristics do you long to possess? What are your greatest priorities?

Then, filter your weight-loss goals through that lens and see if it changes.

GRACE IN ACTION:

Today is a blank slate. Looking ahead, what is one healthy choice you can make in the name of glorifying God?

DAY 9: IT'S ALL TOO MUCH

VERSE: *For by grace you have been saved through faith. And this is not your own doing; it is the gift of God, not a result of works, so that no one may boast.* Ephesians 2:8-9 ESV

READ: Ephesians 2:4-10

YOU'RE TRYING. Hard. Like really hard.

You want to fix your weight and food problems so badly, but it seems like the harder you try, the deeper you dig yourself in.

More exercise. Less bread. More water. Fewer cookies the size of your head.

There's so much you feel like you "should" be doing, it overwhelms you and you don't even start. I call it Analysis Paralysis.

And, it can happen in any area of your life.

Do you ever feel (or at least act) like you need to earn your salvation, even though you've already confessed your need for Jesus and asked Him to rule and reign in your life? You know you're saved and yet you can't help but feel like you need to do more.

More service. More prayer. More devotional time. More organizing every function your church has.

But, trying to earn favor with God is futile because all the heavy lifting was done on the cross. There's not one iota of anything that your self-effort can add.

Why's this? So that we can show the immeasurable riches of His grace! We didn't deserve it but He did it anyway, and now He gets the glory. Because of His grace, we grow in trust and love in our relationship with Him. And that shines brightly to the lost world around us!

So, how does this apply to your weight and food struggles?

What if the "fix" to your food struggles isn't found in how you eat? What if God is simply using this area of weakness in your life as a canvas for Him to create something beautiful?

Because, in a world that is obsessed with all things beauty and weight loss, one who pursues a better way will shine like a city on a hill.

GRACE IN ACTION:

What would happen if you shifted just 10% of your efforts from trying to lose weight to seeking first the Kingdom of God and His righteousness (Matthew 6:33)?

How can you try that shift on for size today?

DAY 10: MISSION: POSSIBLE

VERSE: *"In the same way, let your light shine before others, so that they may see your good works and give glory to your Father who is in heaven."* Matthew 5:16 ESV

READ: Matthew 5:13-16

FOOD, it seems so harmless when compared to other areas of temptation. When we push past that inner eating check in our spirit that tells us we've crossed the line, it's so easy to justify-- after all, it's not like we're cheating, stealing, or bursting from irritation at the painfully slow checkout clerk.

What we eat feels personal. It's our thing and it doesn't affect anyone else.

Or does it?

As a Christian, the world around you is your mission field. You don't have to be a full-time missionary to have an area of influence. Your city, your neighborhood, your street, and your household are watching you.

And, believe it or not, how you interact with food says something about who you believe God is.

Do you believe that...

...God is your provider and that He'll meet all of your needs according to His riches in glory (Philippians 4:19)?

...the Holy Spirit deserves the name Comforter (John 14:26)?

...the Lord will heal your broken heart (Psalm 147:3)?

OR, do you turn to food to try to manage your concerns and meet your needs?

Freedom has a fragrance – and when you walk in it, those around you will be drawn to you (2 Corinthians 2:15).

Be relieved...because I'm not talking about eating perfectly-portioned, so healthy it's "holy" food. I'm talking about making choices with God in mind, even if it doesn't play out as beautifully as you'd planned.

You see, not many people willingly subject themselves to emotionally and physically difficult challenges. But those who do, draw us in.

WHEN YOU CHOOSE to keep going even when you want to wave the white flag, it speaks volumes to the value of Christ in your life.

When you get up one more stinkin' time, when it would be so much easier to stay stuck in the mud, it screams, "He is worth it!" to the world.

How you eat has to do with so much more than you. You set an example in word and deed to those around you, and even your struggles can be used for His glory!

GRACE IN ACTION:

Today, it's time to focus on how you can tell others about the goodness of God! This need not involve how you eat (but it could). The idea is simply to get our eyes off our plates and onto the harvest.

DAY 11: HE BRUSHES THE CRUMBS AWAY

VERSE: *For all have sinned and fall short of the glory of God, and are justified by his grace as a gift, through the redemption that is in Christ Jesus.* Romans 3:23-24 ESV

READ: Romans 3:21-28

HOUSTON, we have a problem. You and me, we're in deep doo-doo.

No matter how hard we plan, pray, and promise ourselves we'll do better, we're destined to fail. And I'm not talking about missing your husband's birthday or forgetting to pay a parking ticket kind of failure.

Nope, we're talking about really serious stuff. The stuff that keeps us out of the Lord's presence, eternally.

Are you shocked? God sure isn't. The Bible tells us that even when we were still sinners, Christ died for us. Our all-knowing God is not limited by time. Your life exists in the same space of His knowledge as the death of His Son.

WHILE YOU WERE YET SLICING off paper-thin slivers of leftover chocolate cake until it was gone— Christ died for you.

✓ Every time you turned to food instead of God— it's washed away.

✓ No matter how many diets you've blown on Day 1— they're ancient history.

✓ Every crumb of "evidence" left on your cheeks— He's brushed them away.

BUT DO you act like it?

Why is it that we so often tie our identity and value to our food failures?

Our negative assessment only leads to further guilt and shame, which have a sneaky way of growing into (even more) poor choices. It's a joy-stealing cycle that can only be stopped by one thing.

So, how can you stop the downward spiral? With God's grace. Grace that washes and wipes away our human failures.

Instead of meeting your less-than-awesome moments with frustration, put on praise. Think about what God has done for you!

No matter how far you fall into the marshmallow fluff, He loves you more than you can comprehend.

GRACE IN ACTION:

Today is Salvation Celebration Day! Spend the day thanking God for sending His Son, and thanking Jesus for doing that which not one of us could do. Then, praise Him with your choices and in your failures (as they remind you of how He's covered you with His blood).

DAY 12: WHY YOUR FOCUS MATTERS SO MUCH

VERSE: *For I consider that the sufferings of this present time are not worth comparing with the glory that is to be revealed to us.* Romans 8:18 ESV

READ: Romans 8:18-25

"THIS IS SO HARD," I said to myself as I resisted a second serving of cheesecake. I didn't need it. My belly was full and I'd had a wonderful dinner. But, I wanted it. Bad.

Self-denial. Ugh.

It felt like my inner toddler was going to jump out of my skin and plunge her chubby little cheeks into the center of those remaining 3 slices, regardless of who was watching.

That cheesecake was all I could think about and....I forgot to remember the after. The "is to be."

Can you relate?

Have you ever noticed that you can take a small craving and nurse it into a gigantic "I need that NOW!" one?

We humans have the gift of imagination, but the ability to visualize and dream can also turn our desire into an insistent distraction.

The problem is that we're focusing on the wrong thing. We're romanticizing the food and forgetting about the "after."

The after can sing or stink depending on what choice you make.

Paul knew a thing or two about this. He even called his struggles, marked with prison and bloody beatings, "light and momentary affliction" (2 Corinthians 4:17).

What would happen if rather than focusing on the food, you thought about how amazing you'll feel when you wake up tomorrow, having made a choice you're proud of? How would it change your perception of suffering and your experience of joy?

Where you focus, matters.

GRACE IN ACTION:

When the desire to eat outside of your true body's needs pops up today, notice what you're thinking. Are you making resistance harder on yourself by thinking about the food and not the Father? Try shifting your daydreaming from the goodies to the "glory that will be revealed" in you!

DAY 13: WHY YOUR MOTIVATION MATTERS

VERSE: *Do not be conformed to this world, but be transformed by the renewal of your mind, that by testing you may discern what is the will of God, what is good and acceptable and perfect.* Romans 12:2 ESV

READ: Romans 12:1-2

"HAVE YOU LOST WEIGHT?" you hear as you're rushing through the door, almost late for church. But those words, they're enough to stop you in your tracks. They are a choir of angels to your ears.

You've been trying so hard and someone is finally noticing! Now it's all worth it. Or is it?

Why do you want to lose weight? While we may say that our purpose is health and happiness, there's a good chance we're being influenced by the media and marketing messages around us. The world promotes weight loss as a near solution to all of life's problems.

Lose weight-- the men will want you and the women will envy you. You'll get the job, find your passion, and magically have a perfect sense of style. You'll be praised, admired, and, essentially, glorified.

Wow, do you see how contrary these motives are to God's ways?

Our purpose is not to shine ourselves but to reflect His glory. We're called to build one another up, to be part of His body, and to walk in purity.

> **Surface-y, selfish motivations don't settle with the Spirit within us, and their foundation is shaky when faced with an assault of the delicious sort.**

If you find that your motivation to eat well and move more wanes when tempted or when results are slow, then consider how you could upgrade your purpose in your health and fitness pursuits.

GRACE IN ACTION:

What are your top 3 goals? Do those goals motivate you to action even when the going gets tough?

Consider how you can deepen your "why" into the spiritual realm, so that you don't feel dependent on external props for your progress.

DAY 14: IS YOUR EATING "GOOD ENOUGH"?

VERSE: *Are you so foolish? Having begun by the Spirit, are you now being perfected by the flesh?* Galatians 3:3 ESV

READ: Galatians 3:1-6

CALL me the teacher's pet if you like. I own it. For much of my life, I measured my worth as a student, employee, or whatever-I-was-doing not by being good enough but by being the best. I'll admit that even a B has brought me to tears. What a shame.

Striving and unrealistic expectations are mean step sisters that can steal the joy out of just about any area of our lives.

Our faith and eating are no exceptions. When we try to earn our salvation, we're walking according to the law and missing out on all that Christ has done for us.

When we first accept Jesus, it's often because we see the divide between our sinfulness and God's holiness-- we realize that we're incapable and are desperate for His grace.

But then something happens. We begin to move from accepting the gift to trying to earn it. Maybe you see it in your perfect church attendance or the way you feel guilty when you miss your Bible study.

Either way, this type of thinking can seep into your eating too:

You eat a (second) donut and wonder how God could possibly be happy with you.

You commit to making a change and try really, really hard, but a bite turns into a bender, and you wonder how God could ever bless you.

You try and fail and figure He must be frustrated.

You're trying to earn God's favor with your eating. You're walking in the law with food. The law that destroys... But the Spirit, the Spirit gives **LIFE** (2 Corinthians 3:6).

If your eating is draining your joy and drowning you in condemnation, it's time for a grace check!

- *Are you trying to earn God's favor by eating well?*
- *Is condemnation a familiar feeling?*
- *Do you believe your actions are more impactful in God's eyes than Christ's?*

GRACE IN ACTION:

Take some time today to examine your thoughts about God and your eating. How do you think your "good" and "bad" food days alter His opinion of you and His blessings on you? Then, determine if your automatic thoughts are true or false based on the Word of God.

DAY 15: "CLEAN EATING" FOR COOKIE LOVERS

VERSE: *"Do you not see that whatever goes into a person from outside cannot defile him, since it enters not his heart but his stomach, and is expelled?" (Thus he declared all foods clean.)* Mark 7:18b-19 ESV

READ: Mark 7: 14-23

YEAH, WE WENT "THERE." What you eat (or what you leave on your plate) just ends up in the trash. It doesn't become part of who you are or speak to your worth or value. However, if you come from a dieting past, chances are good that you've come to adopt a way of thinking about food that is causing you a lot of grief….

"Good" and "bad" food labels. You have them and could probably create a seemingly countless list of "healthy" and "unhealthy" foods. While it is true that some foods are more or less beneficial, the quality of our meals was never meant to be a measurement of how good our day was, how lovable we're allowed to feel, or how interested God is in hearing our prayers.

Jesus declared all foods clean because the endless food rules brought upon His people by the Pharisees were weighing them down and distracting them from what really mattered. Sound familiar?

These unnecessary labels bring baggage with them-- and not the kind the airline can easily lose (although that would be nice). Because of this, you probably find it hard to stop eating those "bad" foods, especially if it feels like they ruined your good eating day. You may even keep going, vowing to start afresh tomorrow, meanwhile gasping for those last bites of the chewy cookies you love.

But, somehow, tomorrow looks a lot like today. And, the cycle continues.

To put a stop to this spin cycle, we keep trying to perfect our eating-- but it's a set-up to flop. The only way to get off the hamster wheel is to ditch your diet labels and accept God's unending grace that even drowns out food disasters. This is true "clean eating!"

GRACE IN ACTION:

Today, pay attention to how you label foods or the way you eat. Notice how these thoughts affect your choices. Do they make moderate eating harder or easier?

Consider how dropping those labels could help you feel less tension around your food choices. Tomorrow, we'll dig into how healthy eating fits into this mix.

DAY 16: GRACE IS A HIGHER STANDARD

VERSE: *So, whether you eat or drink, or whatever you do, do all to the glory of God.* 1 Corinthians 10:31 ESV

READ: 1 Corinthians 10:28-31

I KNOW what you're thinking. If you stop labeling foods as "good" or "bad," you'll sustain yourself on pizza, brownies, and mocha frappuccinos with extra whip (no lid, please). You can almost feel yourself gaining weight. And what about your health?! It's not pretty and it scares you.

But this thought process misses one very important point. While all foods are "clean," we're called to a higher standard than external food rules. While it may feel like you're giving yourself too much slack by ditching your food labels, you're actually setting a **higher standard** for yourself.

The law says "do not kill"-- but Jesus says to not even harbor anger in your heart. Ouch!

It's MORE, not less.

God is calling you not to clean up your outside by following a food plan or by losing weight with white knuckles. Nope, He wants you to live for His glory because you love Him. Nothing more, nothing less.

How does this translate into your daily eating decisions? If all foods are clean, but you want to glorify Him in your choices, what on earth should you eat?

It depends.

It depends on how the Spirit leads you. We do know that it probably doesn't mean bingeing on Ben & Jerry's or skipping meals to make restitution for going bonkers at a buffet.

It likely looks like making moderate food choices between hunger and fullness, and enjoying dessert with your husband on date night, or eating some cookies your kids made for you. It may mean partaking of something "fattening" your Auntie serves for dinner, while politely taking home dessert because you're full and secretly putting it in the trash.

There are no rules, only the prompting of the Holy Spirit.

GRACE IN ACTION:

Before you eat (at least once today) pray for the Holy Spirit to speak His will into your heart. It may not be super-obvious, and you may need to tap into your God-given wisdom of what's godly action, but the beauty is in the try. I know that your trying touches God's heart!

DAY 17: WHAT BUILDS YOU UP?

VERSE: *"ALL THINGS ARE LAWFUL,"* but not all things are helpful. *"All things are lawful,"* but not all things build up. 1 Corinthians 10: 23 ESV

READ: 1 Corinthians 10: 23-27

WHAT DO you do when you **know** there are certain foods you "shouldn't" eat? I'm talking to the woman whose doctor just told her that she "must" avoid carbs or the gal who wants to join her church in a New Year's fast.

You're learning that you have freedom in Christ and you long to glorify Him in your body, but the very fact that certain foods are kept at arm's length is making you feel like a toddler in the candy aisle. You can't have it...and now you want it more than ever.

You feel deprived and then guilty for wanting that which hurts you. It's a lose-lose situation and you're looking for a way out.

The answer to your wavering is not found in picking a side-- and living in total abstinence or hedonism. Nope, relief is found in embracing your freedom of choice. No matter how hard your doctor shakes his finger at you or how deeply the Spirit echoes within your heart, you're still completely free to eat as you please.

Just as we're free to skip a mortgage payment or speed like Fast & Furious on the highway, we make decisions (and choose consequences) every single day. The decision and its outcome are in our court.

This realization has been life-giving to my journey. When I embraced my freedom of choice, I began to make better choices. No longer was I "restricting and bingeing" or eating like a health nut in public, only to act like a garbage can in secret. I knew that I could eat what I wanted, when I wanted, and that allowed me to tap into my true wants and needs.

To this day, I'll walk down the cookie aisle or skim a restaurant menu and remind myself that I can eat "whatever I want." It's my choice and my outcome.

GRACE IN ACTION:

What drives your eating choices? Today, pay attention to your thoughts and actions, then try to estimate how many decisions are made mindfully (what you want and need) or reactively (in compliance or rebellion to what you think you "should" eat).

DAY 18: WHEN FOOD IS "TOO GOOD"

VERSE: *But put on the Lord Jesus Christ, and make no provision for the flesh, to gratify its desires.* Romans 13:14 ESV

READ: Romans 13:11-14

YOU ZOOM into the grocery store to pick up some tomatoes and onions for tonight's chili. But, to get to the produce department, you have to walk smack dab through the middle of the bakery (not cool, people, not cool). There the aroma of freshly baked cupcakes sounds eerily like a cry to come home with you.

Then, you thought about the last time you brought cupcakes home and how you vowed to never bring them home again, as you ate the last vanilla and neon blue bite.

Surely this time will be different, you thought. After all, you'd been doing so well with your eating.

Cupcakes meet cart.

> **How short our memories can be. When something we desire is at stake, we tend to downplay the problems while making optimistically unfounded predictions for the future. We make provision for the flesh.**

What are those foods and situations that are a total set-up for you? Whether it's a specific type of food, an emotional state, or a time of day that's problematic, it's wise to make provisions for and with our spirits.

While ridding the house of M&Ms can feel like a diet, it's good to remember that you don't "have to" stop eating colorful choco-late candies. But, can you decide to make a kind choice for yourself (in light of the Word of God), just for today?.... It's never always and forever.

There are plenty of amazing and incredible foods that you can prepare and enjoy that are good but not "too good." As you improve your skills and strengthen your spirit, you'll be better able to navigate the foods that tend to hobble you now.

And someday, those cupcakes will go stale on your countertop.

GRACE IN ACTION:

Take a look around your pantry. Are there any foods in there that trip you up? Can you temporarily remove them from your home or store them out of sight?

Think about any foods that you'd label "too good" to have around the house, and consider taking a break from them while you work on your relationship with and your reliance on the Lord.

DAY 19: ARE YOU LEAKING WATER?

VERSE: *For my people have committed two evils: they have forsaken me, the fountain of living waters, and hewed out cisterns for themselves, broken cisterns that can hold no water.* Jeremiah 2:13 ESV

READ: Jeremiah 2:9-13

OUCH. If you feel like you just visited the woodshed after reading that verse, you're not alone. We tend to shy away from discipline because it stings. But, it's important to acknowledge our sin...because she who is forgiven much, loves much (Luke 7:47). And we both know that a love for God is the antidote to our food struggles.

Imagine living in Biblical times. You're headed home from your early morning trip to the well when you feel a droplet of water tickle your arm. Your water pot has a leak. Sigh. You know that throughout the day that drip, drip, drip is going to be draining your refreshment.

Such is the case with our eating. What would you do for food? I mean, to what lengths would you go to spend time with the pastries or pizza you love?

If you're anything like I was, you'd squander your hard-earned money, look forward to time away from your family (so you'd have time with your food), and get everything just right for the "moment" you get to eat.

Sounds a bit like being in love, doesn't it?

So, what do you go to food for? What is it that you expect and seek in that relationship?

Do you long for comfort, pleasure, or a reward? Are you seeking stress relief, time to zone out, or just a moment to silence the demanding voices around you?

If so, you've got a broken water pot, my friend. You're trying to find soul refreshment in that which was never intended to contain it. Now, our incredible Savior doesn't rub our noses in our sin. Instead, He asks us to agree with Him that our plan is far from leakproof (repent), move on, and stop camping out in our sin (John 8:11).

If you feel bogged down in your sinful ways with food, do not allow it to put a wedge between you and God by keeping your eyes on your faults and giving ear to your negative self-talk.

Allow Him to provide you with His vessel of refreshment-- and allow your need for Him to grow your love.

GRACE IN ACTION:

Consider how you will transfer your effort and admiration from food to God, and make a plan to do it at least once today!

DAY 20: ARE YOU "GUILTING" YOURSELF TO DEATH?

VERSE: *For godly grief produces a repentance that leads to salvation without regret, whereas worldly grief produces death.* 2 Corinthians 7:10 ESV

READ: 2 Corinthians 7:8-10

REGRET. **I'd say it's my least favorite feeling.** I despise laying my head down on my pillow only to replay the things I'd done that I wish I could forget.

While to many it may seem trivial, those midnight musings often centered around food in my life. I'd start out the day with fairy-tale expectations only to crash and burn like a giraffe trying to run across ice.

And my harshest critic was myself. I thought that if I felt bad enough, that if the guilt were sickening enough, then finally I'd stop the madness. Then, I'd be repentant.

But guilt never delivered. Rather, it left me feeling like a garbage bag on the curb after missing trash day. I was "stinky." And all those around me could smell the negativity too. My attitude and shortness were proof positive that guilt leads to death.

> *On the other hand*, **the ways of God bring us to life and light. God does not shame us or leave us naked. He clothes our sin and grants us repentance** (2 Timothy 2:24-25).

Did you catch that? He — God the Father, Son, and Holy Spirit — convicts us of sin and gives us the gift of repentance.

I think we're all pretty familiar with the fact that we can't earn salvation, but we often forget that godly grief is a work of the Holy Spirit. If you find yourself trying to muscle up repentance by harvesting guilt— STOP!

The enemy will only use your efforts to put a wedge between you and God. Turn his plan on its head and choose to pursue the Lord, in prayer, asking Him to plant a seed in your heart, so that you hate your sin the way He does. Then, cozy up on the pillow of His lap— the place where His love will cultivate your heart.

GRACE IN ACTION:

What is the role of guilt in your food life? How is it helping or hurting you? The next time you feel like the solution to your problems is "feeling worse," step back and determine which course of action will help you move away from food and to the Lord.

DAY 21: THERE WHEN YOU NEED IT MOST

VERSE: *Let us then with confidence draw near to the throne of grace, that we may receive mercy and find grace to help in time of need.* Hebrews 4:16 ESV

READ: Hebrews 4:14-16

WHEN DO you feel most comfortable, even confident, approaching God? At what times do you feel a little more sure that He hears your prayer or answers your plea?

Even though you may be familiar with this verse and believe that God is attentive to His children, chances are you hang your head low when you feel steeped in your weaknesses. I get it. That's how we live our human lives-- we're used to having our stellar performances met with praise and our undesirable idiosyncrasies given the cold shoulder.

But as the heavens are higher than the earth, so are His thoughts higher than our thoughts and His ways higher than our ways (Isaiah 55:9). God doesn't stockpile His grace for when you're enjoying a season of smooth sailing. Nope.

Jesus came here and lived in this crazy world we call our temporary home. And, because He understands how hard it can be on our disintegrating planet, He sympathizes. His heart is with us and His grace is for us.

Take a moment and read our verse again, taking note of **the time** He suggests we draw near with confidence...

Hint: It isn't the time you feel self-assured. Not when you're up-to-date on your Bible reading plan, or after you've passed out tracts on a hot afternoon, or when your hair is looking divine.

We're admonished to sprint to God in moments of need. And not with our tail between our legs, friend.

Like a child who hurts herself by doing the very thing she knew she shouldn't have, she runs into her father's arms for comfort and to mend her wounds.

In the same way, we can approach God. Not because of what we have done but because of Christ who "passed through the heavens," came out victorious, and made us children of God.

Jesus has made provisions for you on "those" days. When you feel your worst and you need God the most, you can be confident that you'll receive mercy and find grace to help in your time of temptation.

GRACE IN ACTION:

Whether you were blessed with loving parents or not, consider what unconditional love looks like. What does it mean to have no strings attached to adoration? What would it feel like to know you always had a safe place to land? How could this affect your relationship with food? Determine one way you can begin to walk in this assurance today.

DAY 22: DESPERATE TIMES CALL FOR...

VERSE: *And there was a woman who had had a discharge of blood for twelve years, and though she had spent all her living on physicians, she could not be healed by anyone.* Luke 8:43 ESV

READ: Luke 8:43-48

HOW MANY THOUSANDS have you spent on diets and "expert solutions" to your food problems? From therapy to diet pills and books, no doubt I've shelled out tens of thousands of dollars.

And it felt like the more money I sank into these solutions, the more I sank. Not because I wasn't trying. I was. Hard. But because it seemed like no one person or program could fix me.

Boy, was I right!

I can relate to the woman in this story we read today. She put so much into her healing, she fixed herself poor. She was desperate and had no other options. That is, until Jesus came onto the scene. There was something special about this (God) man and she could sense it. All of her past failures and disappointments had to be shed so that she could press in harder than the rest of the crowd.

She was so confident in His ability to heal her that her only desire was to touch the hem of His garment. And despite the odds, she made it to The Solution to her pain. Immediately her faith had made her whole. Jesus felt the power of God transfer from Him to her, and both knew something had changed.

What do you desperately press into in your moments of distress? What would happen if you put the same amount of effort into seeking the hem of His garment as you do into pursuing food?

For those of us who feel chewed up and spit out by diets and our feeble attempts to reel in our eating, it would change everything. Your problems are not too big or too small for our Lord. He is waiting for you to reach out... so that He can show up like no other can.

GRACE IN ACTION:

What would true desperation for His help look like in your life? Determine a plan of action that's not dependent on you, and decide how you'll press into Him the next time temptation hits.

DAY 23: WHEN FOOD STARTS TO STINK

VERSE: *Those who cling to worthless idols forfeit the grace that could be theirs.* Jonah 2:8 NIV

READ: Jonah 2

"HE SMELLS LIKE SOUR CREAM," my 3-year-old daughter said as she clung to her "Grayson," the lovie she held on to during bedtime, as she refused to wash him. His hair is matted and his seams weakening and yet-- he is her most valued possession.

I imagine if I ever attempted to tear him from her arms, it would be an epic battle filled with tears and unprecedented acts of toddler strength. I dare not be so cruel. Even as an imperfect parent, I love her too much and would never want to cause such distress.

And maybe, just maybe, I can also relate.

I remember the first time that I went on a diet. I cried to my mom, mourning, "Food is all I have." **I was desperate to lose weight, but I could hardly bear the thought of letting go of that which I adored most.**

For years and years, this same thought rattled around in my mind, causing me to make some rather detrimental food decisions. I was clinging to food-- even though it had turned like the milk you don't even want to uncap to pour down the sink.

Like a little girl holding on to her ragged bear, the little girl whose arms are locked and unwilling to let go, I held on. Can you relate?

> **What we are missing is our Father, waiting with open arms, ready to embrace us with grace, if...we'd only let go.**

Are you clinging to food? Maybe diets and restrictions have left you guarding what's "yours." Or, traumatic experiences may have caused you to look for comfort in the fridge. Either way, your arms are closed and unable to experience what true comfort, true relief, and true nourishment are.

It's ok if you're scared to let go. Remember that His perfect love casts out fear (1 John 4:18).

GRACE IN ACTION:

What's one reason you cling to food? How can God meet that need? Look up scriptures to fill the true need and write it on a note to carry with you today.

DAY 24: THE STRUGGLE IS REAL

VERSE: *And he said to all, "If anyone would come after me, let him deny himself and take up his cross daily and follow me."* Luke 9:23 ESV

READ: Luke 9:23-27

THEY SAY, "THE STRUGGLE IS REAL." Being a wife, mom, and disciple can be hard. Especially on the days the washer breaks, the car won't start, and we're faced with a pint of chocolate brownie ice cream at the end of that day.

The struggle is real because that's the way it's meant to be. **To struggle without purpose is torture. To struggle with purpose is exactly what Christ did and directs us to do.** And, I know it seems trivial to compare your desire for an Oreo to the cross, but let's look at the bigger picture here. The cross was Christ yielding to God's plan.

We are encouraged and equipped to do the same when we look to the cross. Food freedom comes not because He fixes us but because we fix our gaze. If you're struggling today, be reminded of what the cross really means to you!

I used to wish that I could swap out my food challenges with something I could quit. You know, detox from or swear off for good. But, God had bigger plans for me than that.

How about you? Do you ever wish you could trade in your desire for donuts? Have you ever questioned why God hasn't delivered you despite your frequent requests?

He, my friend, has a greater purpose for you.

The struggle is real because God wants us to rely on Him DAILY to overcome.

GRACE IN ACTION:

Today, choose to proactively struggle for the sake of Christ. Toss the most (or least) amazing bite from your plate, exercise when you'd rather lie comatose on the couch, or swap a pastry for a prayer. Then, celebrate and meditate on the joy that comes after walking in His footsteps.

DAY 25: HE DID IT FOR THE SOUP

VERSE: *"Look, I am about to die,"* Esau said. *"What good is the birthright to me?"* Genesis 25:32 NIV

READ: Genesis 25:24-34

"I'M SO hungry I'm going to D-I-E!"

Ever said it? Or at least thought it?

Yes, it does seem pretty dramatic. But when our emotions are running high, it sure can feel that way.

Take Esau for example. We read his story in Genesis 25. He was out working in the field and came home ravenously hungry. He found that his brother, Jacob, had made a yummy soup. Esau demanded that Jacob share with him.

But Jacob, he was sly. He offered to trade the soup for Esau's birthright. (Essentially, his place as the oldest, the first heir of his father's wealth.)

And Esau, deciding that his hunger was the most important thing IN THE WORLD, agreed.

This is a story you wouldn't believe to be true if it wasn't in the Bible.

Esau was so overwhelmed by his hunger he did something crazy. Totally insane. He gave up everything he had.

For lentil soup, friends! We're not talking about double-decker brownie fudge ice cream here. Just some soup.

Have you ever felt crazy over a food choice? Like me, you may find this story to be a consolation. However, chances are that we both can relate on a much deeper level.

Have you ever sold the promises and provisions of God in your life for food? Have you ever forfeited His grace, His comfort, or His direction...for the sake of a meal?

Our Heavenly Father has so much more for us if we will just wait for it.

GRACE IN ACTION:

Today, wait on God before eating. It doesn't matter how short or long you go, but do so with quiet anticipation of how He will meet your deepest hunger.

DAY 26: THE PERILS OF PERFECTIONISM

VERSE: *"Come to me, all who labor and are heavy laden, and I will give you rest."* Matthew 11:28 ESV

READ: Matthew 11:25-30

"LOSE 10 POUNDS IN 7 DAYS!" the checkout magazine boasted. You couldn't help but pick it up and flip to page 19, since the woman ahead of you had just as many coupons.

Your eyes scanned the prescribed food plan and then your queue of purchases. Not. Even. Close. You made the best choices you could, and yet, you were miles away from steamed spinach and trout.

"If this is what it requires to do it right, I'll always be wrong," you thought-- and you tossed a candy bar onto the grocery belt.

When the bar is too high, we stop trying. This is why you've struggled with diets.

At one point you thought you could do it ALL, tomorrow. But time has revealed to you (and 95% of dieters) that change does not happen overnight. And ironically, striving for a perfect diet only makes it harder to eat healthfully, as our cravings grow fangs when our favorite foods are banned from our lives.

Yet, to fix the problem, we continue to apply the same "medicine" that made us sick in the first place.

So, what's the solution?

GRACE. Grace in your eating means giving yourself room to be human. It means understanding that you won't nail it, but trying anyway because you're grateful for all God has done for you. Grace on your plate means not letting slips turn into slides and getting back up (rather than rolling around in the mud).

Grace is The Solution.

GRACE IN ACTION:

Take today to meditate on how grace can and will transform your life and your eating. What would happen if you stopped aiming for perfection and set your gaze on God's goodness instead? How would things change if your food slips "go and reset" as soon as you noticed you'd veered? The answer may surprise you!

DAY 27: WALKING TO A DIFFERENT BEAT

VERSE: *"They are not of the world, just as I am not of the world."* John 17:16 ESV

READ: John 17:6-19

THE WORLD TELLS us to lose weight to be a better version of ourselves. If we lose those unwanted pounds, we'll be healthier, happier, and more confident.

And it's ok to want to lose weight and to gain all of these things. But if you find these desires crumbling like the coffee cake topping you can't get off your mind, then it's probably because you're not of this world.

You, my sister in Christ, walk to the beat of a different drum.

The beating in your heart is not fueled by selfish ambitions but by the very blood of Christ. You want more than an "extreme makeover" of the external sort. **You want to impact the world because of all He has done for you** (even if your flesh doesn't know it yet).

If you want to make your weight-loss goals meaningful, look beyond the scale and see those in your immediate influence. How would being healthier help you reach and serve them?

Now, gaze beyond your four walls. What're 1,000 steps or 1,000 miles in your radius that fires your motivation to move more and move past your cravings?

This is lining your goals up with those of the Father. Can you feel the difference?

When you can expand your vision and your goals, you'll start to see the ripple effect of putting your health at the forefront. Then, you'll be tapping into the Rhythm that'll echo deep within your spirit to propel you further than you've ever gone before!

GRACE IN ACTION:

Dream BIG! What would you do for Christ if no-thing stood in your way? Now, tie your health and fitness goals into that vision.

How would being a more fit and energetic version of yourself help you accomplish your calling?

DAY 28: THE SCARIEST PART OF CHANGE

VERSE: *"Be strong and courageous. Do not be afraid or terrified because of them, for the Lord your God goes with you; he will never leave you nor forsake you."* Deuteronomy 31:6 NIV

READ: Deuteronomy 31:1-8

CHANGE IS SCARY.

Uncertainty causes our minds to wander in fear and anxiety, making predictions of peril and unrest.

Why is it that we're so good at pulling out the worst possibilities in just about any scenario?

Call it crazy or call it a survival mechanism but definitely call it out.

Because often, the scariest thing about change is "our fear of it."

Take your desire to make different food choices. What keeps you making the same unwanted decisions over and over again? What do you imagine it'll be like if you say "no" to that 10 pm ice cream that seems to melt away the day's stress? I suspect it's not pretty. You may see yourself tormented with the desire to eat as if you were sitting in a pile of red ants. That is scary!

But, what's the truth here?

Have you done hard things before? Ever taken care of a child with the flu while making trips to the bathroom every 15 minutes yourself? Ever studied for exams until even a double espresso wouldn't keep you awake? Ever given birth?

You can do crazy-difficult things, my friend. Things that make skipping the sugar cravings look like a trip to Disneyland.

It's all about whether you nurse the fear of change OR **you nurture your confidence that the Lord will never leave you or forsake you.**

What kind of story are you telling yourself?

GRACE IN ACTION:

Just as the Israelites created memorials to remind themselves of all that God had done for them, take some time today to rehearse (and write down) all that God has seen you through. Then, when faced with a temptation, recall the stories of His great faithfulness.

DAY 29: IT'S A JOY!

VERSE: *"Count it all joy, my brothers, when you meet trials of various kinds."* James 1:2 ESV

READ: James 1:1-8

TRIALS.

Also translated as troubles, testings, and **temptations**.

The pull you feel toward the chips and queso (extra queso, please) is meant to cause joy. Not angst, frustration, and shame. JOY!

Why joy? Because in verse 4, we're told that these things will ultimately lead to us being "perfect and complete, lacking in nothing."

The very thing you may despise about yourself is probably the very tool that God is using to make you more like Him.

He can and will use your food struggles to accomplish something really, really great in your life. Like, "I wouldn't trade this for the world" great.

And, that's why He calls us blessed because of it (v12).

The enemy wants you to run away from God in embarrassment and shame when you're struggling. He wants you to feel too dirty to go into His presence. He'll even convince you that you need to clean yourself up first before going to Your Father.

But, you've been trying to clean yourself up with a diet for far, far too long. Even our best efforts fail because we were never meant to be the "changers" in our own lives. God created you-- and He wants to be the one to guide, direct, and clean you (even the crusty queso on your chin).

Stop feeling like a failure and start acting like His precious child. Put aside the thoughts about who you're not and fill your heart and mind with who He is.

That is how you "receive the crown of life, which God has promised to those who love him." (v12)

GRACE IN ACTION:

Today, be a thought detective and notice every negative thing you say about yourself. Then, swap out that thought with a verse from the Psalms about who He is!

DAY 30: THE PURPOSE OF YOUR DELIVERANCE

VERSE: *[God,] who comforts us in all our troubles, so that we can comfort those in any trouble with the comfort we ourselves receive from God.* 2 Corinthians 1:4 NIV

READ: 2 Corinthians 1:1-11

THIS WHOLE THING. It's about so much more than your waist size, blood pressure, or even your food freedom.

No doubt, you want to feel confident, healthy, and peaceful. But, God's omnipotence won't let Him stop there. He has a grand plan and you are a very important part of it all.

As you've learned through this devotional, our struggles are meant to point us to Him. Our weaknesses are to remind us that

He is strong. And our daily failures, well, they're part of the human condition.

When we embrace this new, grace-filled way of thinking, our lives change. We walk a little lighter, even if the scale hasn't changed one iota. We have more peace and a greater sense of purpose. We shine!

You don't need to be a size 6 or a "clean" eater to be used by God. The only requirement is that you share what you've been taught (that's witnessing!) and what you've been given (that's serving!).

The purpose of your deliverance is not about the temporal but the eternal.

The purpose of your deliverance is the salvation of others.

The purpose of your deliverance will make every tear you've shed and every pound you've mourned more than worth it.

God has an amazing calling on your life, sis, and this is just a taste of it!

GRACE IN ACTION:

Act "as if" today. God transcends time and He sees you walking in freedom, even now! With that knowledge, make one (or more) choices today that reflect that truth, and do so with the purpose of your deliverance in mind!

AFTERWORD

Congratulations on completing *Grace Filled Plates*!

Chances are the concept of giving yourself grace is foreign, and the thought of giving yourself grace in your eating...well, it's alien.

But as Christians, we are foreigners, aliens, in this world. And, it's not too surprising that God would do things the complete opposite of the status quo.

So, if you're feeling a little unsure, that's a good thing...

Diets may have been familiar-- but they made you miserable. Let's trade in that familiarity and misery for HOPE. Hope for change is **always** alive in Christ!

As you continue your journey, I invite you to catch up with me at **GraceFilledPlate.com** - you'll find real encouragement and practical tips to keep your progress coming. See you there!

ACKNOWLEDGMENTS

This devotional is truly God-penned. Not that I'm special in hearing His voice. Quite the opposite. I'm ordinary as ordinary can be. But, the Lord has seen fit to put the most incredible people in my life, and to them and Him, I am eternally grateful.

To my Heavenly Father. You've used the most unpleasant circumstances in my life as the most transformational, so much so that I wouldn't trade them for anything in the world!

To my "G & G," my late grandma and grandpa. Your hard work and the gifts you left each of us grandkids was how I was able to start Grace Filled Plate. Grandpa, you worked so hard, with only your family in mind. Grandma, your faithful work at the daycare and the money you tucked away for us behind the pictures in your office have been used to impact thousands of women. Thank you!

To my incredible husband, Doug. You have truly shown me unconditional love and grace, and you've helped me grow into a person that I'm happy to be. You are the most amazing husband and father!

To my priceless daughter, Raegan. You are more precious to me than a million words could communicate and I am grateful the Lord has allowed me to be your mom.

To my parents. I'm thankful for your unconditional love and support. Mom, for making innumerable sacrifices to put my best interests first. Dad, for working long hours to make all of it even possible. Mom, thank you for your essential help with Grace Filled Plates and your endless enthusiasm for everything I do. Love you two!

To my mother-in-love, Felicia. I'm forever indebted to you and your efforts in raising the most amazing man of God. Thank you for sitting with me in some of the hardest times in my life and for being such an integral part of Raegan's life. Your help has made Grace Filled Plate and this book possible.

To those who have encouraged me by sharing the blogging journey with me: Lisa at Coffee and Keyboard, Amy, Ginger, Jeni B, and countless others.

To my readers. Your prayers and encouragement are a treasure, truly light and water to the seed of Grace Filled Plate that God has planted in my heart.

Printed in Great Britain
by Amazon